HAL•LEONARD VIOLIN PLAY-ALONG

ELEMENTARY CLASSICS

CONTENTS

ISBN 978-1-4584-1920-0

HAL•LEONARD® CORPORATION

7777 W. BLUEMOUND RD. P.O. BOX 13819 MILWAUKEE, WI 53213

In Australia Contact:
Hal Leonard Australia Pty. Ltd.
4 Lentara Court
Cheltenham, Victoria, 3192 Australia
Email: ausadmin@halleonard.com.au

Visit Hal Leonard Online at
www.halleonard.com

Air

Gottfried Finger (1660-1723)

Air

Henry Purcell (1659-1695)

Andantino

Wolfgang Amadeus Mozart (1756-1791)

Bourrée

George Frideric Handel (1685-1759)

Deutscher Tanz

Joseph Haydn (1732-1809)

Ecossaise

Franz Schubert (1797-1828)

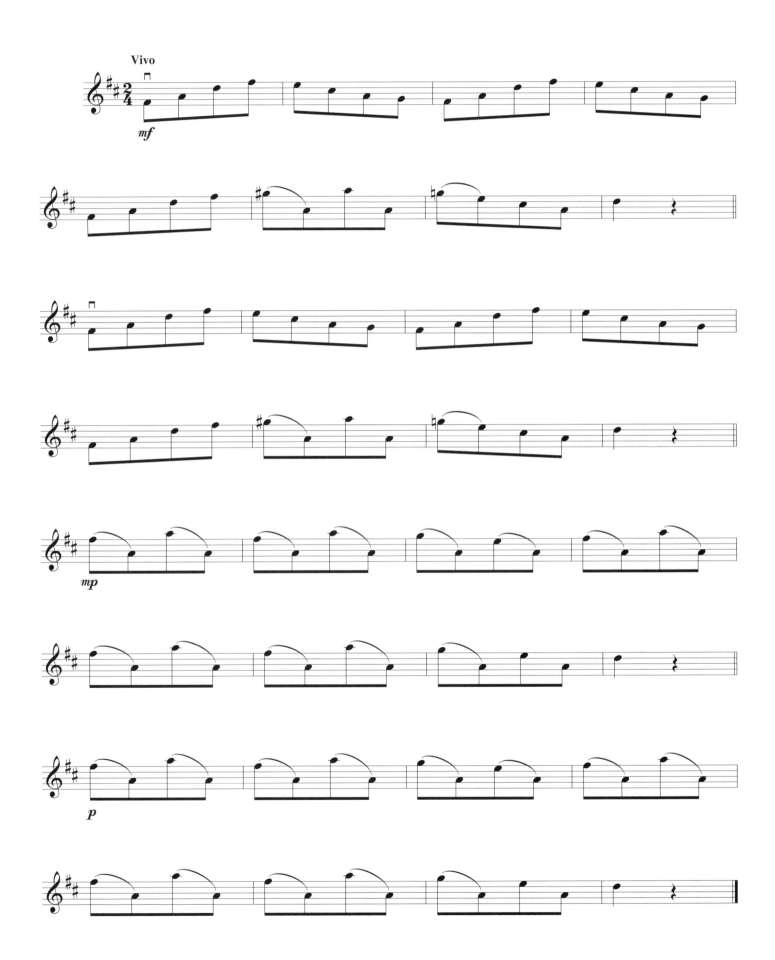

Fröhlicher Tanz

Christoph Willibald Gluck (1714-1787)

Gavotte

Giovanni Battista Martini (1706-1784)

Moderato

J'ai du bon tabac

Traditional

Lied

Johannes Brahms (1833-1897)

March

Robert Schumann (1810-1856)

Menuet

Jean-Baptiste Lully (1632-1687)

Menuet

George Philipp Telemann (1681-1767)

Waltz
Carl Maria von Weber (1786-1826)